Marine Painting

IN OIL AND WATERCOLOR

STANLEY WOODWARD

Marine Painting

IN OIL AND WATERCOLOR

THIRD EDITION: REVISED AND ENLARGED

BONANZA BOOKS

Library of Congress catalog card number 67-10334

This edition published by Bonanza Books,
a division of Crown Publishers, Inc.,
by arrangement with Watson-Guptill Publications
b c d e f g h

Printed in Japan

Dedicated to my daughter, Patricia

"Nature I loved and next to nature Art."

WALTER SAVAGE LANDOR

Publisher's Note

AMONG THE several traditional subjects that appeal to the painter, none exerts a stronger feeling of mystery and beauty than the sea. There is an exciting challenge in the movement of waves, whether subtle or violent, and the shifting effects of light that fascinate nearly all artists, amateur and professional.

It is no wonder then that the marine paintings of Stanley Woodward have such an enthusiastic audience. Few contemporary painters of the sea can evoke its moods with such technical mastery and imagination. And certainly few marine artists can communicate so well the essentials of their craft to the non-professional painter.

This guide book, revised and expanded from Mr. Woodward's earlier, highly successful *Marine Painting in Oil and Watercolor*, not only instructs the aspiring marine painter in the technical elements of a compelling art, but will help, we feel, to engender in him that special love of subject that distinguishes the successful marine artist.

Preface

ONE SUMMER in Rockport, Massachusetts, where I was conducting a painting class, I answered a knock at my studio door. There stood a middle-aged lady burdened with a fragile easel, a tiny paint box, and a sun umbrella. Breathlessly she confided her ambition to become a marine painter—she wanted to learn how to paint big, slashing canvases of tumultuous seas. She was positive I could help her. No, she had never painted the ocean but she was sure she could because she simply adored it. When I inquired how much time she could give to the fulfillment of such a laudable purpose, she replied that she could only stay in Rockport two weeks because she had to return home to get her daughter ready for school.

I am sure that, among readers who have taken up this book, none regards painting of marines as casually as that. Neither do I expect many to pursue the subject as fanatically as did the late Charles H. Woodbury, a painter of magnificent marines, who, on one of his West Indian voyages, commanded the sailors to lash him to the steamer's side in a gale. From this unusual viewpoint, looking forward, he painted the vessel careening in the mountainous seas.

Somewhere between these two extremes the beginner can

set his goal and chart his course. I have introduced the subject here to make it plain at the outset that this book is considerably more than ten easy lessons for the dilettante. The art of marine painting, like that of landscape or portrait painting, is a serious undertaking that yields only to patience and perseverance. But if I had not believed that I could be of considerable help to purposefully-minded students, I would not have taken up my pen. I have tried here to demonstrate my own working methods. Other painters doubtless proceed in different ways, but the best that any teacher can do is to give the benefit of his own experience. So this book may perhaps be considered an account of my adventure in marine painting, as well as an invitation to adventure on the part of those who are irresistibly drawn to the sea.

There seems to be a general opinion that it is more difficult to paint the ocean than the land. Indeed I have observed that many good landscape painters do not find it easy to transfer their dry-land skills when they attempt to paint the sea. The marine painter cannot copy his subject as can the painter of hills and meadows—not that the best landscapists do exactly that, but their subjects do stay relatively still. Studying the forms and action of water might better be compared to studying the human figure in motion. In both situations the trained eye and the analytical mind first acquaint themselves with the desired action then record it on canvas creatively. Once the artist has learned how water behaves under varying conditions, he need not pray that the waves be still long enough for him to copy them as he might copy a photograph.

Important as it is to acquire usable knowledge of wave and surf forms—these might be called the anatomy of the sea—there remain the bigger aspects of composition, color, and dramatic effect; these constitute the *art* of painting. For that, precisely the same kind of creative ability is needed as for the painting of any other type of subject. However, since the experience of painting the sea may be new to readers, I am demonstrating in these pages how I attack the problem. Those who follow my procedure may discover, in learning, another and better approach after a time. Painting is, after all, an individual problem, and every success in art is a personal triumph of original thought, personality, and character. The teacher can only direct the learner's steps until he is well on his way.

Most artists are linked to a chain of artistic thought and expression. In my formative years, Winslow Homer, Charles H. Woodbury, Paul Dougherty, and Frederick Waugh were potent influences. Each of these men was a great painter of the sea; all of them spent most of their lives depicting it; each had a different story to tell and an individual way of telling it. To students interested in becoming marine painters, their works provide a point of reflection and study as compared to the student's own efforts that are inspired by the sea itself. Of these men, Homer has had incomparably the greatest influence, not only upon marine painting but indeed upon American art, and he is the most highly regarded. Waugh was the great realist, his pictures showing the highest degree of skill in their fidelity to nature. Woodbury, a man of profound intellect, approached the subject of marine painting in a scientific manner, and he successfully conducted a school of painting the greater part of his life. Dougherty at his best was in the front rank of all marine painters.

It is to be expected that you who undertake this adventure in marine painting will suffer many discouragements. None of us is immune to failure, no matter how far along we seem to have traveled. I can think of no more disheartening an experience than to return from an afternoon's painting on the rocks, broken in spirit, feeling utterly frustrated, realizing how far short of one's high hopes the accomplishment has been. But these dark hours pass and are forgotten in the thrill of future successes. There is nothing so soul-satisfying as, when you lay down your brushes and take one last lingering look at a really good sketch, you realize that at last you have "got something." You know you have. You know it deep down and nobody has to tell you.

One thing you must possess—that is a love of the sea. The more fanatical your devotion, the better. Years ago, my wife and I, on our honeymoon, were leisurely motoring through the mountains of New Hampshire. We had got as far as Bethlehem when storm warnings were received on the radio. That was like the sound of alarm to an old fire horse. In imagination I saw the waves filling the cove, envisioned the spray, white against the rocks at my Ogunquit, Maine, studio —over two hundred miles away. Should we turn and dash for the coast? The answer was yes. It was a momentous decision, and we never regretted it! The studio, lashed by rain and racked by wind, was waiting for us, and so was the surf, giving me a priceless opportunity for study and work.

I mention this episode to point up the marine painter's passion for the sea in all its moods—and they are infinite. Color and action change with the wind, the ebb and flow of the tide, the time of day or night, the direction and intensity of light, the condition of the sky, the density or clarity of the atmosphere, even the geographic location and, of course, the painter's viewpoint in relation to the horizon. To become acquainted with these manifestations of one of nature's most dramatic elements is the fascinating adventure of marine painting.

STANLEY WOODWARD
Cape Ann, Massachusetts

Contents

Marine Painting
IN OIL AND WATERCOLOR

ONE

Painting Equipment

AS MARINE PAINTING is largely an outdoor affair, it is of the utmost importance to have equipment especially suited to the rugged work it entails. Avoid a fragile easel that can be easily blown over by the wind or that is difficult to adjust to uneven ground. One that is too cumbersome or too weighty is not practical either, as in nearly every case the easel, together with paint box and canvas, has to be carried over dangerous footing among the rocks.

The Anderson type easel, formerly made in East Gloucester, Massachusetts, is admirable. I have used one for over twelve years with constant satisfaction. This easel permits the paint box, with palette in it, to rest within easy reach just below the canvas, leaving one hand free to paint while the other holds the extra brushes and paint rag. It is necessarily very sturdy but it is not too burdensome to carry slung over the shoulder like a musket: an important consideration because, even today when we travel so much by motor, the artist has to do considerable walking in search of subjects. In bygone days, when we all walked more than at present, light equipment was especially important. Years ago I painted for several summers

THE CONFLICT *(30 x 36) Action is the keynote of this painting. Consider what is taking place: In the distance, the big seas are making up and rolling in; half of the foreground wave has crashed as the other half, drawn into the vortex of its forward movement, is about to follow suit; the foreground foam is in uneasy motion seeking to level off and, from the rocks to the right, excess water still cascades over the edges and pours through the crevices between. So much movement, in fact, takes place in the water and rock areas that the sky purposely has been left plain to keep all the interest below it. The gulls are very necessary to the composition, as their downward directional line points to, and helps accentuate, the focal point of interest of the painting. It is interesting to note that the structural lines of the composition are based on the triangle.*

on Monhegan Island off the coast of Maine, where automobiles were nonexistent. Most of the paintable subjects were on the farther end of the island at least two miles from the hotel. Because of the distance, I carried only the necessary equipment, especially as a lunch box had also to be taken along.

I have emphasized the necessity of a good workable easel for outdoor work, but it should be understood that its use is intended only for canvases larger than those that are carried in a sketch box. When painting on the 12″ x 16″ panels that fit my sketch box, I sit on the ground with the open box in front of me and with the painting panel inserted in the cover, thus dispensing altogether with an easel. As I believe in being comfortable and at ease when at work, I have for years carried

THE AUTHOR PAINTING ON THE MAIN COAST *Equipped with paint box holding a 12″ x 16″ canvas, the author is shown making one of the innumerable firsthand studies of the sea and rocks which continue to furnish the basic material for his finished pictures. The photograph shows how close to the water's edge the box is set and how comfortable one can be when a cushion is substituted for a boulder. Note the panel which, although set in the groove on the left side, overlaps the front of the box cover on the right. This allows complete freedom of brush strokes and permits the artist to draw his brush stroke right up to and off the edge of the canvas.*

with me an old automobile cushion which has proved to be a great comfort when seated on hard New England granite.

There are advantages to be gained for the marine artist in painting from a sitting position. Setting up an easel on the uneven rocks is difficult; it is far easier to get nearer the action of the sea when we have only ourselves to worry about. Then again, the wind is much less apt to wreck one's equipment, as often it is possible to get in the lee of a friendly boulder that protects one from both the wind and rain. More important than all these is the advantage of a low eye level from which the oncoming waves assume greater height and the rocks and cliffs seem mightier in proportion. In consequence, the picture's composition is bound to achieve greater dramatic force.

For me, the sketch box holding 12" x 16" canvas boards has proved most useful. Such panels are as small as I care to work on in oils and yet are large enough to allow free handling of the brush. The larger the canvas boards, the bigger the box must be to contain them and so, again, practical considerations have a way of intruding.

My marine studies done on these 12" x 16" sketch boards might well be called the basis of my finished paintings. But just now we are considering them only in the light of working material. They consist of cotton canvas mounted on cardboard; two or three at a time can be carried in the cover of the paint box—a valuable point on a week-end painting trip. These panels can be purchased in most standard sizes up to 25" x 30", but in the larger dimensions they are apt to buckle and therefore are not too practical. If I require a painting surface above 20" x 24" in size, I prefer a stretched canvas. I do not like absorbent canvas, so I usually cover these canvas boards with one or two priming coats of white lead or "Sani-flat" before using. "Sani-flat" is the trade name of a preparation made by the Benjamin Moore Company.

Quite often, especially when I am painting in a tropical or semi-tropical country, and know that I may have to stand in the direct sun, I stain the surface of the painting ground with a thin coat of umber, burnt sienna, and raw sienna. The surface thus darkened avoids unpleasant reflection of the sun's bright glare. I squeeze a bit of each color onto the canvases in varying combinations, apply a large brush soaked with turpentine, and paint the whole surface with it. After a minute or two of drying, I take a rag and rub the canvas evenly over the entire surface. As I do not use the same combination of pigments each time, or in equal quantities, the result is a variety of canvas boards ranging in color from dark mahogany brown to light brown-red. If the canvas has a slight tooth, all the better; it makes for a beautiful texture.

With or without the dark canvas, I have long since got used to painting in the sun, preferring to set the canvas with sun-

STANLEY WOODWARD'S BRUSHES *These well-worn brushes have been used by Woodward for many years. Reading from right to left, the smallest brush is an outline brush; numbers 4, 5, and 6 are used most for sketch-size canvases; numbers 7 through 11 are employed for larger canvases.*

light full upon it rather than in the shadow against the light. But if the sunlight is on my canvas it must also be upon the palette. Time was when I thought I had to have a sun umbrella, as did most of the other students in my group. The incident which changed my mind happened in this manner: One day after a morning spent painting on the rocks, I was walking back through the village of Ogunquit to keep a luncheon appointment with Ed Pothast, a fellow painter. As I hurried along the street, carrying paint box and easel in one hand and umbrella with smock inside it in the other, I thought that I smelled smoke, but looking about I could see no evidence of a conflagration. I entered the restaurant, hungry and tired, and finally located Pothast, who was talking with the proprietor. I thought Ed looked at me rather queerly. Grabbing my arm he said: "Woodward, the boss says if you are coming in here, to kindly take that fire outside." "What fire?" I asked. Looking down, I saw that the inside of my umbrella was a smouldering mass. I rushed out and opened it up. Only a circular rim

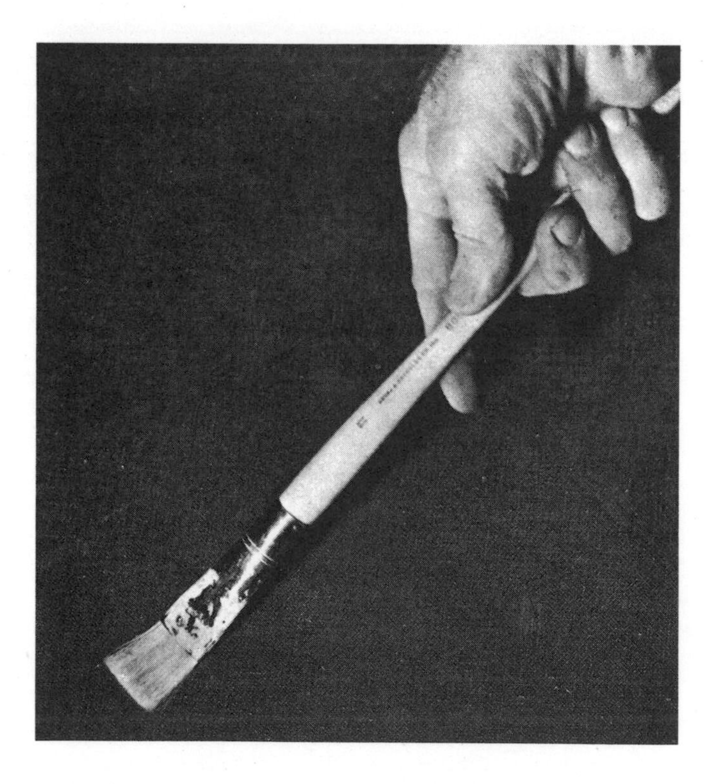

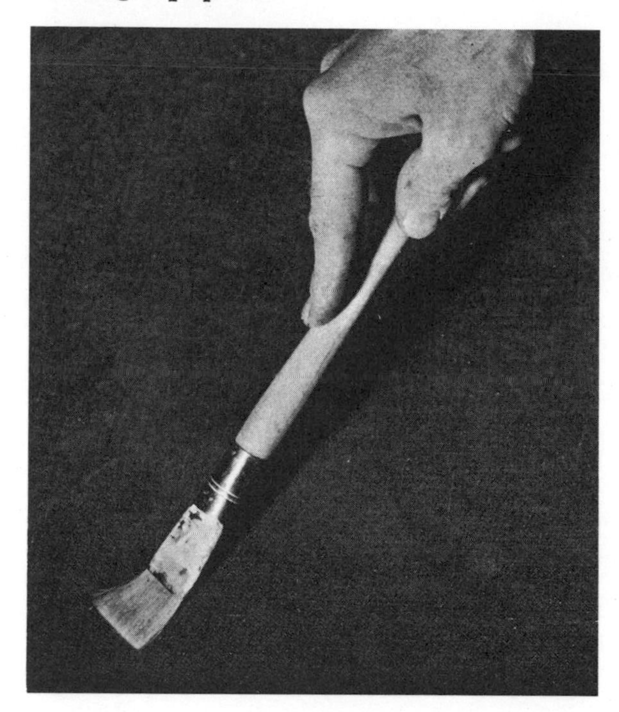

For vigorous painting the brush should be grasped firmly in the hand as one holds a hammer, with the thumb uppermost on the handle as shown.

of fabric remained; the center had entirely burned out, and half of the smock was consumed too. Ashes from my pipe must have fallen into the closed umbrella, and I had walked for at least a mile through town carrying the incipient blaze. I have never used a sketching umbrella or a smock since!

Referring once more to painting surfaces, I might say that I have made frequent use of the so-called "academy board" made of pressed wood. Unless cut to a narrow gauge, it can become very heavy, especially in the larger sizes. But it is durable and can often be purchased when canvas is not available. One side is rather smooth, too smooth in fact; the opposite side is too rough. In preparing the boards for painting, I first shellac the smooth side as a filler. When it is dry, I apply at least two coats of white lead or "Sani-flat." Before allowing the last coat of white to dry, and in order to get away from the smooth, slippery surface, I press the back of some spare linen canvas to the wet paint. When lifted quickly, it imposes the texture of the canvas upon the board. However, nothing can take the place of the give and spring of canvas when properly stretched. Because the firm, unyielding stiffness of the board has a tendency to alter my technique, I prefer to paint with the palette knife instead of the brush, at least on sizes above 20″ x 24″. This is no hardship, as I enjoy the peculiar quality that the palette knife gives. Anything that adds variety and enriches one's art experience is valuable.

Pigments, as they come from the tubes, are often too stiff to use directly without a thinning medium. A fifty per cent mixture of turpentine and linseed oil has been my usual standby. But I like to experiment and, for a change, employ a mixture of oil and varnish (sixty per cent linseed oil and forty per cent damar varnish). Varnish dries quickly and has a tacky quality which aids in building up a surface texture that can be obtained in no other way.

The rather short, flat bristle brushes known as "brights" are admirably adapted for outdoor marine painting. I have used and found entirely satisfactory those identified by the Rubens trademark, and also the Mussini brushes. They come in many sizes, but numbers 3 to 9 should take care of all needs except when painting on very large canvases. By turning the brush edgewise, it is possible to produce a thin line. For vigorous painting, the brush should be grasped firmly in the hand as one holds a hammer, with the thumb uppermost on the handle.

The proper care of equipment is essential to top performance in any medium. The figure skater relies on keen steel blades, the tennis player on a firmly strung racquet, the carpenter on a razor-edge chisel. To the painter no less important are his brushes and an orderly, clean palette. We go to great trouble and expense to select the proper brushes and the best colors, and yet it is sometimes appalling to see a student neglect both. Failure to wipe clean the mixing surface of the palette and to clean the brushes after the day's work can almost be termed criminal neglect.

On this subject the words of Robert Henri, the great painter and teacher of other years, are eloquent: "You must know your tools. You must have the best, and they must be in perfect

Photograph by George M. Cushing, Jr.

THE AUTHOR IN HIS STUDIO, ROCKPORT, MASSACHUSETTS
Stanley Woodward paints on an easel that has an unusual history. Made in Munich, Germany near the end of the last century, it became the property of various artists, many of whom took the easel along with them when they moved from place to place. In the upper left-hand drawer is recorded, by each artist, the story of the easel's travels to date. "When I purchased it in 1921 from Eric Pape and brought it to the Frederick P. Vinton Studio in Boston where I lived," says Woodward, "the records showed that the easel had already journeyed from Munich to Hamburg, to Paris, Cairo, London and Edinburgh. The last entry, my own, is dated Rockport, Massachusetts, 1936."

arrangement for service. Painting requires great judgment and skill. In the effort to capture and record in paint one's sensations there must be no handicap with the materials. To be negligent, to be above such mean things as the materials one handles, to be a sort of genius in a dream is a common misconception of our artist's state. The technique of painting begins with the simplest mechanical issues and extends through to the heights of science."

Over the years I have found that the simplest and best method in the world for cleaning brushes is with plain soap and water. A piece of soap held in the palm of the left hand, warm water running from the faucet—plus a little "elbow grease"—are all that are required.

TWO

Colors

I DO NOT WANT to be dogmatic about the choice of colors that should be on the marine painter's palette. The choice is one that varies with the individual artist and is subject to change even with him as his art progresses through development of new ideas and techniques. He experiments with colors as he does with ideas. Along the way, he picks up additional colors which have proved their worth and discards others which appear to duplicate or which he has learned to do without.

Although I have always had for ready use a rather full palette, I am aware that many painters prefer to limit themselves to a few pigments, claiming that this practice makes for unity, simplicity, and harmony in a painting. I can think of Goya's rather meager palette and of the handful of colors that Anders Zorn is said to have used. But new colors have a way of cropping up in these modern times, and some have proved very useful to me for certain kinds of sea painting. Therefore I can see no good reason for not availing myself of them. When I first began to paint, we had cobalt blue, manganese or turquoise blue, and monastral blue. Cerulean blue (of the finest grade only) I have found to be extremely valuable at all times, but if I were painting in the tropics or in southern waters, as at Nassau, Puerto Rico, or around the Gulf of Mexico, I most surely would have with me either manganese or turquoise blue.

Such brilliant pigments and kindred synthetic hues of both blue and green are dangerous to use in excess and for all occasions. Because of their easily recognizable tints or shades, their too frequent use by a painter in his work becomes more of a trademark than his signature itself. This abuse of any single synthetic tint or hue must not be confused with an artist's frequent tendency to react more sympathetically towards warm or cool tones, or specifically to some primary color.

I have written elsewhere that I am supposed to be somewhat blue conscious, having a predilection for its use, even painting my preliminary outlines in that color. This, no doubt, is inevitable in view of much painting of the very blue waters of the Gulf. The identification of a painter's work with some color tendency is not unusual, but it is not the same as identification with a manufacturer's special color variation. Chauncey Ryder, in his masterly use of green in many of his canvases, is said to have evolved a brand of his own which we young painters admiringly referred to as "Ryder green." Charles Burchfield, the watercolorist, certainly has explored the possibilities of gray tones far more than the average painter in his successful attempt to render their subtle variations. It is certain, though, that you cannot squeeze a Ryder green out of a tube, nor yet a Burchfield gray. These are synthetic expressions of the painters themselves.

It will not be necessary for me to take up the different pigments and discuss each separately. A chart is given listing them all. I want to mention a few because they are related in various ways to our special subject. I have always been partial to a certain zinc white. Although I have painted at one time or another with most other whites, I have always returned to the Rembrandt brand. This is not necessarily because it is better—I do not know enough on that score to risk an opinion—but only that it suits me, especially its degree of pliability as it comes from the tube; painting out of doors is no time to bother with a stiff paint requiring a lot of medium.

It is curious that for many years black was never on my palette, mostly for the reason that I was warned early against its use out of doors. The advice is clearly disputable. I have discovered that it is indeed quite a useful color. The mixture

THE AUTHOR'S OUT-OF-DOOR PALETTE *The inevitable state of his palette, as with much use and daily wiping of used area, the pigments gradually encroach on available mixing surface. The hardened paint can be removed with paint remover from time to time. A good idea is to give the newly purchased palette a thorough rubbing with linseed oil before using.*

Woodward uses the following colors, though not all at one time. Those on his palette at any given time depend upon the nature of the work in hand.

1. *zinc white*
2. *zinc yellow*
3. *cadmium yellow, medium*
4. *cadmium orange*
5. *cadmium red, lightest*
6. *yellow ochre*
7. *raw sienna*
8. *burnt umber*
9. *burnt sienna*
10. *rose madder*
11. *alizarin crimson*
12. *viridian*
13. *cerulean blue*
14. *cobalt blue*
15. *manganese*
16. *ultramarine*
17. *indian red*
18. *black*

of ivory black and cadmium red, for instance, produces a splendid, restrained violet, shadow-like tone. I have found that mars violet, which is not included in the average palette, is useful in obtaining certain desirable effects in my moonlight pictures.

The beginner often asks the artist how he gets a certain color, meaning what combination or mixture of pigments produces a particularly subtle shade which seems so right. Nine times out of ten, the artist would not be able to say just how. He knows what color variation he wants, and the means to obtain it lie in the various pigments on his palette. If you know what color you want, you can mix it. One has first to learn to see color, and the rest is easy. It is entirely a question of visual perception improved by practice, and not a chemical formula to be memorized.

Very rarely in oils, except in underpainting, are colors painted directly on the canvas as they come from the tubes. An attempt is made to mix the desired tone, and if the eye and mind perceive it to be there in error, other colors are added until the result satisfies. Some painters achieve a result in one way, others could possibly attain the same tone with quite a different admixture of paint. The manner in which it is accomplished is unimportant. And the answer as to what color it should be can stem only from the painter himself.

The interest in the particular palette of any great artist can only be an academic one on the part of another, since, even when the list of pigments the great one uses is known, it does not reveal the secret of their transformation through the brain and hand of the artist.

Summing up the question of pigments and colors, it is improved by constant practice and through the experience gained by observing and recording nature's color relations, while the ability to mix the desired color grows always apace.

THREE

Some First Problems

IT IS SO EASY to magnify the importance of details in ocean painting. It's the marine student's biggest bugaboo. He seizes on a detail—a wave, or some part of it—and attempts to paint it. Naturally, before he has even mixed the color, it is gone. This disappearance confuses him. Having been used to painting landscapes, he is accustomed to the tree and the stone wall standing still. He has to take an entirely different approach now. Let us look at it in this way. This wave is only a detail in our picture. At present it is not even an important detail. It is a part, and a small part, of a larger mass of water, and this larger mass is only one of several component parts of the whole pattern of the picture.

This mythical wave of ours, with its own shape, form, color, and position, is not a fixed and immutable thing to be studied, dissected and painted as of itself. It cannot be divorced from its origin—the surrounding waters and the force that gives it movement. Hence we do not and cannot look at it, even in nature, apart from that from which it springs. Neither do we paint it so. Once we have learned this basic fact, we can then

STRAITSMOUTH LIGHT *This canvas (25 x 30) was painted in the studio after Woodward had made a 12" x 16" oil sketch out of doors during a November storm. It is not a mere enlargement of the small sketch, which, however, did record the needed facts of color, movement and mood of the stormy seas. In constructing the larger picture, changes were made in the structure and composition of the rocks of the foreground; the lighthouse was moved nearer to the center of the picture and, as an added item, the gulls, which in the sketch were clustered about the extreme point of land, were given a directional line pointing downward from the upper right-hand corner as a balance to the slanting rock ledge at the left.*

relegate the wave to its proper place in the scheme of things as a whole.

It goes without saying that the more thorough our knowledge of wave structure and action, the less worried will we be about this when we begin work on a canvas. I always advise students to supplement their painting with innumerable pencil studies; I suggest that they make careful drawings of a breaking wave at different stages of its brief rise and fall. No two waves are exactly alike, but if you are patient enough, after selecting the moment you wish to record, you will find that approximately the same action will take place in succeeding waves. Much practice with pen or pencil in this manner will, in time, enable you to anticipate what will happen, your strokes will gain in accuracy and force, and the quickness of eye to observe and hand to record will become a habit.

The accompanying preliminary sketches I made with a felt-tip, commercial package marker pen. It is very useful for quick and vigorous impressions, and I have used this type of pen

PRELIMINARY BLACK AND WHITE DRAWINGS *Each of these drawings of "Chapins Gulley" in heavy surf is an attempt to produce a different composition from the same local area by means of choosing a different climactic moment of the breaking surf and also by changing somewhat my own relative position in the cove. To the layman they might seem very similar, but to the artist, using them later as reference, each design presents a new and different problem to be solved.*

This is a quick line drawing of a breaker or comber, emphasizing its sweeping rhythm and force as it nears the shore.

since its introduction. There is one drawback, however: It will not erase; each stroke is final.

When a great wave breaks over the rock guarding the cove, the whole area within is momentarily filled with a swirling flood of white foam. After a few seconds it gradually levels off and soon the white is broken up into ever enlarging cir-

A study of Bald Head Cliff, Maine. As can be seen, little detail is involved in this sketch, only the position and movement of the great wave as it rushes into the narrow channel and crashes high up on the cliff. The cliffs and foreground rocks are put in as simple dark areas, while the backwash and turmoil surrounding the outer ledge are briefly indicated. The dark cloud suggests a storm motif.

cular and elliptical shapes, usually of a light green color. As you look at these rapidly changing forms, intricate and beautiful in design, you despair of getting even their approximation down on canvas. Now look again, but this time try to view the cove in its proper relation to all else in the picture; that is, the sky, the distant water, and the rocks. Considered under these conditions, the cove appears to all intents and purposes only as an irregular mass of near-white bounded by dark rocks. Thus viewed, it is clear that all these intricate patterns have lost their former importance and will not, after all, have to be so carefully painted to gain the desired effect. It is only necessary that this large area preserve its general light value and that here and there upon it a few characteristic shapes and movements be suggested. If the plan of my painting calls for a sizeable area of light foam or surf nearly white in value, I usually let my bare canvas serve for this as long as possible. I am always amazed when I get around to painting this area at how few details are required. It all tends toward simplification, a very desirable quality.

Such ten or fifteen minute studies, like this one of surf breaking against rocks, cannot hope to supply all the information necessary for future paintings, but doing them will help to get the student to recognize and to quickly lay out on paper or canvas the large important areas of his marine.

In selecting a position from which to paint, it should be borne in mind that the nearer you get to the level of the ocean, the higher and bigger the waves will appear. From this low vantage point in heavy surf, the seas will often obscure the horizon, and the sky become their background. It is all in the point of view. The same degree of surf viewed from a higher level appears less impressive.

These and other considerations determine the structure of

THE LEDGES, WATERCOLOR *(24 x 30) The special problem here was one of rendering moving water meeting an unrelenting wall of rock and the resultant impact produced. The water in the foreground is painted directly on a slightly damp paper. The white areas are the original paper itself. The cliffs and foreground rocks, however, were built up to their present dark values by repeated overpainting, first allowing each previous application to dry. The white paper was allowed to work for me to the last; consequently the foreground rocks were laid in early.*

MOONLIGHT ON PEBBLE BEACH, WATERCOLOR *(24 x 30) The magic of moonlight on water is never more striking than when seen from a beach head. Given a clear night, a fair amount of surf, and the full moon an hour or so above the horizon, you will have all the necessary ingredients. This painting reflects the light of a harvest, or golden, moon using a color scheme based on yellows and greens. Note that the sand, though wet, does not reflect the path of the moon, as all the water has run off or been absorbed. Also, sand, in common with grass and trees, has a heavily textured surface with little or no reflecting properties.*

your composition. For instance, how high in your picture will the horizon be placed? The amount of cloud interest may help to determine the answer. If the beauty of the sky is the feature that most interests you, then less space is given to the ocean. Conversely, if the sea is the thing and the sky is a monotone of gray, a narrow strip of sky may be quite enough. Carrying this analysis still further, one can on occasion obtain variety in composition by looking directly downward at the water

HEAVY GOING, OIL *(28 x 36)*
This sailing schooner is one of the last of that valiant fleet which was once the pride of Gloucester, Massachusetts. It is depicted here rounding Eastern Point, Cape Ann in heavy seas. Should you wish to see the original painting, you would literally have to go to jail, as it hangs in the Rockport, Massachusetts police station as one of several paintings donated by local artists when the building was dedicated.

from an elevation. In this case, of course, there is no horizon or sky visible and the form and shapes of the broken surf must be unusually well painted. The following four examples show what effects can be achieved by modifying the composition to depict varied moods of the sea.

LIGHT ON THE SEA, WATERCOLOR *(15 x 18) Here is an attempt to capture fleeting effects of light on water. Since, because of shifting clouds, the light is constantly changing, it becomes a question of choosing the most dramatic moment and sticking to it. The observation and work involved in capturing a single effect is all worth the effort and challenges the painter's every resource. Observe how the heavy cloud just above the horizon throws a long black shadow on the ocean.*

FOUR

Preliminary Studies

In Oil

I HAVE ALWAYS THOUGHT that the best way to learn to paint the sea is to go out and paint it as faithfully as possible. Later, perhaps, we can work more creatively in the studio as we come to a fuller expression of our own personal interpretation. But before we change, idealize, or distort, we must know what it is that we are changing. So let us take our sketch box, go down to the shore and find out. In these on-the-spot sketches, accomplished usually within the hour, my chief aim is to observe and record as nearly as I can the various color relations of sea and sky and land—and, at the same time, their relative black and white values. I do not neglect composition, design, or any of the other elements that go into the making of the picture, but they are not so important in these first sketches and can later be worked out in the studio. The color combinations that nature so generously provides are what I am after. If I can come back with a sketch which seems to have recorded accurately the colors of sea, sky, and rocks on that particular day, at that particular hour, and under the conditions existing at that time, then I have an original color harmony for any use that I wish to put it to later.

After I get these studies home I do not work on them, alter, or change them in an effort to make a picture of them. Those that seem to contain the germ of a painting idea for future exploitation I keep, as well as others which may have in them an unusual sea and sky relation or perhaps an interesting cloud effect; or it may be that I was particularly successful in recording the shape of the spray hitting against the cliff and bounding back. In any case, bit by bit, I have been building up a more complete knowledge of the ways of the sea. Much of this information is recorded in these studies I speak of, but even more of it is indelibly fixed in my mind and memory.

Naturally, as facility increases, the sketches improve both in color and in painting quality. Every few years it has been my habit to cull my vast accumulation of studies, keeping only those which, however rough or meager, contain in them some information of value, at least to me. These firsthand, direct sketches are only a means to an end. Sometimes that end is served when an occasional study becomes the inspiration and working model for a more complete and thoughtful composition on a larger scale. When the resultant painting is made, my interest in that particular sketch is finished. Conversely, I have often refused to part with some recently painted outdoor effort which in my mind's eye already represented a future canvas.

Before discussing these preliminary studies further, it might be well to remark that there is nothing against painting a large canvas out of doors. I would advise the attempt occasionally even for the beginner. It exposes his most glaring faults in a definite manner and makes him realize certain deficiencies in his knowledge, which cannot be glossed over as they might be in a small sketch. Then, too, a feeling of confidence is engendered by working on a large surface with big brushes. There is a certain affinity between the size of the canvas and the immensity of the subject.

On the other hand, there does seem to be a limit to the dimensions of a canvas that can conveniently be painted in the open. When there is any reasonable surf running, there is bound to be a wind blowing, and we have at least four or five square feet of canvas surface exposed to its sometimes devilish machinations. I have found that a canvas 25″ x 30″ is large enough to satisfy the urge to paint broadly out of doors, and it is not too large to be completed at a single sitting. As time goes on, the knowledge gained in making the innumerable studies of previous years unconsciously enters into your thought processes, and while you are apparently attempting to paint the action which goes on before you, much that is put down is drawn from past experience.

In Watercolor

Here is an interesting and productive way to accumulate that store of information relative to the sea, its movement, power, and form, which later will prove so necessary in organizing the studio picture. In the beginning I came to use the small watercolor sketch for reasons of space economy when

PRELIMINARY WATERCOLOR STUDY *This watercolor sketch (the original is 6″ x 8″) is one of many painted along the rocky New England coast. The value of recording quick color impressions of sea and sky lies not only in acquiring a notebook of workable data, but in the training of the eye to see quickly and accurately one color against another, and in putting each down on canvas in proper relation of color values.*

traveling; I found this comparatively light equipment more convenient than oil paint box and canvases, not to mention the brushes that had to be cleaned every day. This was especially true on ocean trips where quarters were cramped and facilities often inadequate. As it turned out, this practice developed into a source of valuable art experience in itself, as, from the very nature of the medium, there were suggested new forms, new ideas, and new color harmonies. Long accustomed to the opaqueness of oil pigments, I found that the transparency and purity of watercolors applied to white paper permitted a greater brilliance of effect than could be achieved in oils. When confronted with the emerald blue water of the West Indies, for instance, watercolors seemed imperative. My watercolor pad for this purpose is a small one, not over six or eight inches in either dimension, and the time needed for a sketch is less than half an hour.

Naturally, one cannot go into much detail in such sketches, but they often suggest complete paintings, containing as they do the broad design of sea, sky, and land with all their particular color relations. Even if none of them actually results in a subsequent finished picture, this constant effort to see color and evaluate the relation of one tone to another, and the rapid recording of the decisions thus formed, is of inestimable value in gaining greater color perception. While on the subject of watercolor, I may remark that I have found it extremely helpful to render in oil a subject first executed as a watercolor and also the reverse. We acquire certain qualities from each medium which we would not get working in one medium alone.

I believe that the fundamentals of outdoor painting can best be learned with oils rather than watercolors. Pursuing this idea a little further, the student who has a thorough grounding in the basic principles of oil is better equipped to try his luck with watercolor. Although watercolor may be a new adventure for him, he will not be starting from scratch, since we assume that color, value, design, subject matter, and draftsmanship have become his familiar tools. What wonderful possibilities lie ahead of him. Uninhibited by a watercolor technique

THE GREEN WAVE, OIL *Courtesy of Esther Burt, Allentown, Pa.*

WATERCOLOR STUDY FOR THE GREEN WAVE

forced upon him by a teacher with a strong personal manner of painting, he starts afresh and cannot fail to evolve through trial, error, and perseverance a method and manner of his own, one so indicative of his personality that his watercolors will have at least one merit—they will be individual. I have found that familiarity with both media is valuable in many ways. Sometimes it happens that one may become a little stale and rather discouraged with oils; a shift to watercolor for a while can help keep alive the enthusiasm so necessary in painting and help to restore a waning confidence. And it may also happen that having once delved into watercolor, an artist may feel so at home and well able to express himself in that medium that he will devote his major efforts to it from there on.

I once saw an exhibition of watercolors by Childe Hassam at the Vose gallery in Boston. I had known him only as an oil painter. I do not know how contemporary critics judged the paintings, but I do know that the memory of their impact on me is still strong. Probably, he took up watercolors only in his maturity. In conclusion, learn in oils, experiment in watercolor. I have profound respect for both.

FIVE

Beginning the Sketch

THERE IS NOTHING very profound in painting an acceptable marine sketch. To anyone who has learned to draw, to see color, and to differentiate values, it should not present more serious difficulties than confront the landscape painter who essays a mountain subject under shifting cloud conditions. In each case an interesting moment is seized which dictates the design of the picture to follow. The landscape painter cannot, at one and the same time, paint the mountain under the shadow of a passing cloud and in full sunlight. A decision must be made. His choice is determined first by the extent of interest aroused in one or the other effect and, second, by his experienced judgment in estimating the chances of this effect remaining long enough to capture it, or of the possibility of its recurring in approximately the same way.

The marine painter who deals with moving forms has many choices as to which movement of changing surf he will utilize for his design. Once he has made up his mind, he is ready to begin. My own method is to proceed to paint in outline the general structure of my composition. That is to say, within the rectangle of the canvas I indicate the component parts of

Photograph by Robert F. Sherman

The author sketching upon the rocky Cape Ann coast of Massachusetts

the picture—the sky, the sea, and the rocks. A further distinction is made in the sea area by separating the deep or distant water from the broken white area of the foreground. This outline usually is painted in blue pigment with turpentine for a medium. If the sun is out and there are shadows on the rocks, it is a great help to paint in the shadow parts at once with the blue tone. It will aid later in marking the distinction between sunlight and shade, and will do no harm, as the shadow areas will be cool anyway. While waiting for the tide to rise a bit and produce the desired surf conditions, it is not a bad idea to utilize the time by thinly painting all rock areas in light and shade, using the blue paint. Later on, when other considerations begin to crowd your attention, you will be glad that drawing the rocks is not one of them. I do not favor the use of charcoal for making this preliminary outline, no matter what the size of the canvas. If one has difficulty in drawing with the brush, this is a good opportunity to acquire the habit. The outline brush should be one of narrow width and should be used for that purpose only.

Assuming that our design is now completed and our pigments freshly laid out upon the palette (with plenty of white on hand), we are now ready to dig in and paint. As the sky sets the tone of our picture, it is painted first. Not too much time should be expended on cloud detail, much of which can be done later, but the value of the sky in terms of light and dark and its general color tone is extremely important, as the rest of the large areas bear a proper and direct relation to it. For instance, when the sky is blue and there are no clouds, the ocean itself assumes a blue shade. With the sky gray, the sea naturally reflects its neutral tone.

Having painted the sky, the distant water area can be set down. This is relatively easy, as we now have something with which to compare it. Is the sea darker in value than the sky, or is it lighter? Is it a deeper blue? Is it warmer in tone, or cooler? Under the conditions already assumed—a cloudless day—the horizon water will probably be much darker in value, and its color blue. Just what shade of blue, and how much modified by reason of distance and other factors, will have to be carefully considered.

We are now ready to devote our attention to the rocks, and we should at this stage cover the canvas with approximately their general color and value as speedily as possible. Since parts of this rock or land area will be painted against the deep water and even the sky at times, we are aided in our estimate of its color relation by comparison with them. For example, the reddish rocks of Cape Ann, on a clear day, usually appear lighter in value than the deep blue of the sea, and certainly warmer in tone.

So far then, we have painted the sky, the distant deep water, the rocks or land area, and we have left a bit of canvas that

BRIAR NECK SURF *Preliminary sketch for rock and sea motif. Painted on the spot, rapidly executed sketches often show more spontaneity and appear less labored than so-called finished paintings. They reflect the painter's first enthusiasm for his subject, unrestricted by any alien demand for a finished product. In spite of crudeness, they remain at their best the complete realization of a positive idea.*

Courtesy of Beverly Hospital, Beverly, Mass.

until now has represented the broken white foam area. Much of this will remain comparatively light, even when we have finished. It is an example of allowing the bare canvas to work for us until the last moment. All that remains is to paint the shape and movement of the breaking wave as it forms out of the distant water to become a focal point of our picture. However, in our outline we have already indicated the moment of action to be portrayed and have more or less confined the limits of that action to a definite space within the still unpainted canvas. This foreground wave will differ in color from the blue, distant sea. The reason is mainly that it is much nearer the shore and of shallow depth and, since it tends towards a vertical plane, reflects much less of the sky's color. In most cases the general color is in shades of green, just what green—whether a cold or warm green—will depend upon conditions that obtain at the time.

Our canvas is now covered, and the eventual worth and distinction of our marine sketch already established by what we have accomplished up to this point. For the first time we can pause and look at it objectively as a whole. There will be many minor corrections to make, emphasis to be directed at the proper point, a few necessary details to be added and perhaps a toning down of nonessential points of interest which distract the eye from the main motif.

Too many students fail at this stage, trying by vain attempts to include everything, only to lose the original freshness, spontaneity, and simplicity which their sketch may have achieved up to this moment.

Adding detail upon detail, they soon become involved in a hopeless welter of confusion, often adding to it by attempting to change altogether the main concept of their original layout. Let well enough alone and concentrate only on the obvious faults!

The foregoing is, in brief, a method of procedure that may help the student to attack his outdoor sketch in a simple, direct fashion. In the following chapter, we shall consider the problem more specifically and, with the aid of color plates and analysis of the different steps taken, we shall demonstrate the actual painting of a marine from start to finish. There will, of necessity, be some repetition of points already covered, but it seems helpful to me to anticipate a detailed exposition by a broad outline of the steps to be taken.

SIX

A Demonstration, Step-by-step

1st Step *The Outline*

THE SUBJECT CHOSEN for demonstration, and shown here in the following color plates, is one originally painted at Ogunquit, Maine. It is typical of the action and color of our New England seacoast and it seemed to lend itself admirably to the division of painting steps with which an attempt is made to show my normal procedure in painting a marine. The mood is a gay one, typical of a sunny day and a condition of light frequently encountered during the summer months in that locality.

The first step is the laying-in of the general pattern of the picture in outline, indicating as simply as possible the distribution of the important masses, such as the sky, the sea, and the land. In addition, we have a further division separating the distant sea and the foreground wave. It is at this point, while deciding upon the structure of the composition, that a most important decision confronts us. What moment or what stage of the breaking wave shall we attempt to render? What moment provides the greatest possibility for dramatic action, considering all the various factors involved? In making this decision we have to consider the probability of the desired action recurring often enough in approximately the same manner for repeated observation.

Referring to the accompanying plate (1st step) it will be seen that I chose the instant when the wave had broken and the ensuing body of foam had begun to cascade forward but had not yet reached the large rock in right center. A few seconds later this great mass of water would reach the barrier of rock, only to be thrown back and upward in a cloud of spray, but that is another story—or rather, another picture.

Continuing with the outline, it will be noted that the horizon line is placed quite high, indicating that most of the action and interest will take place in the lower areas of the canvas. The bottom boundary line of the distant deep water is, in reality, the very important top structural contour of the breaking wave. Once that has been established, we are committed to the form the wave will take in the picture. And hereafter, all other movements of the water, below and on either side, are determined by this decision. The position and general shape of the rocks were next indicated in outline with the same blue color. They appear in strong light and shade; so I have carried them further along than usual as insurance against the sun's failing me later on.

The backwash of water from a previous wave, pouring down from the shadow part of the rock promontory, is very important as a line of movement in opposition to the breaking wave. And by virtue of being in the shadow, and cool in tone, it adds emphasis to the warm whiteness of the foam above.

In the outline stage we must not pay too much attention to subordinate shapes that occur within the broad mass of the foam area. Only the general sweeping movement should be suggested at this point. Too rigid adherence in the beginning to smaller happenings tends to detract from the main movement of which they are a part; indeed, it is apt to be a waste of time because, as the painting progresses, such details will often be found unnecessary or wrongly placed. Notice that in the foam area just above the rocks at the bottom of the canvas,

FIRST STEP *This is a reproduction of Woodward's canvas after he had quickly indicated the general arrangement of masses with blue pigment, greatly thinned with turpentine.*

I have (following my own good advice) merely indicated one or two elliptical shapes and have left the careful drawing of them until later when it comes time to paint them. Not until the canvas is covered will I know just where these details are needed and how many are required.

2nd Step *The Sky*

The outline completed, the painting of the sky was the next consideration. Although in this case the sky does not occupy much space on the canvas, it still is important, as it strikes the keynote in the color scheme of the entire picture. It indicates a clear day with the sun out and everything subject to strong light and shade.

Our color plate of this step shows the sky painted in quickly and with little detail. Clouds are suggested, but not too forcibly, as in this case they are relatively unimportant to the main motif. The line of their movement is quite open to change, as it is often dictated by a need to repeat a similar directional trend of a wave to be developed later on, or sometimes used as an opposing line to complete the rhythm of the picture. We can come back to the sky later.

However, a glance at the color plate of the final step shows that little or no change has been made in the sky area since the original lay-in, as shown in the second step. This brings me to a point that cannot be too strongly emphasized—that of acquiring the habit, by constant practice, of setting down quickly

SECOND STEP *As the sky sets the tone of the picture, it is painted first.*

and accurately the character of the sky. If weather and sky conditions remained constant there would be no need for speed, but this is rarely the case. A wrong guess on the part of the painter to choose the aspect most favorable for continuous effect too often results, let us say, in an attempt to complete a half-finished "gray-day masterpiece" in a flood of sunshine.

In our example here, fortunately, I had no such problem to contend with, but the positions of the clouds in the sky were changing constantly and they disintegrated entirely before the sketch was done.

The value of the sky as a whole is light, and it will be observed that even the shadow parts of the clouds are not appreciably darker than the blue of the sky, their difference being mostly one of color.

The following pigments were used to make this first painting of the sky: cerulean blue, zinc yellow, rose madder, yellow ochre and cobalt blue.

3rd Step *The Distant Water*

Since the ocean reflects the color of the sky above, we know that some shade of blue is inevitable. We now study very carefully the color relationship of the sky and distant water; the relative values too, for the right value is as important as the right color. As a rule, the distant water area does not vary greatly in color or value from top to bottom. When viewed from a low eye level, it appears as a narrow strip of dark sea.

If the prevailing tone is blue, I have found that by modifying the blue with purple toward the horizon, the perspective effect of the sea's limitless expanse is simulated. In the color plate, next page, it will be noticed that far out to sea few details of wave forms are discernible. The ocean near, or at the horizon, seems flat and almost calm, but looking closer to the middle distance, certain definite wave forms begin to take shape and substance. In a very rough or choppy sea these tops of waves will show white caps.

THIRD STEP *In painting the distant water, its value is compared with the sky which has already established a key for value relationships.*

As the waves approach us, the spaces between parallel crests progressively widen until the nearest wave breaks to form the central focusing point of the picture. Only the two or three waves back of the white foam section are clearly defined. In painting the unbroken water of the deep sea, invariably the troughs of the sea facing the sky on a parallel plane reflect its generally light tone. The upturned portions of waves appear darker.

In painting the distant sea area, cover quickly that particular segment of canvas in the approximate color value; then, while the paint is still wet, suggest with the thin edge of the brush the darker tops of the waves and white crests, if any. Next, with the wide part of the brush, bring down the sky color into the troughs between them.

Finally, note that the strong localized green of the large wave in the center appears less intense in the wave just behind, and scarcely at all in the one behind that. Cobalt blue deep, cerulean blue, alizarin crimson and viridian were the colors used in painting the distant sea.

4th Step *The Foreground Wave and The Rocks*

IT WILL BE SEEN that much progress has now been made. The rocks are painted in their approximate colors—warm orange and reds in the sunlight and cool dark purple tones in the shadow. The cool shadow effect was obtained by using alizarin crimson, ultramarine blue, Indian red and a little raw umber. The various shades of green to the left of the foam of the big wave have been noted and hastily set down.

The motion of the wave's upward surge in a sort of "S" shape is suggested, and the general design of the foam patterns, which show the action, have been blocked in. Lower down, the sweeping back surge of water in the shadow of the central rock has been given a cool lavender tone. Immediately below, the broken water above the foreground rocks was next covered with a light emerald green tint. My endeavor at this stage of the game was to brush in quickly the remaining unpainted sections of the canvas—to establish their approximate values and colors—in order to arrive at the point where I could look at my canvas as a whole and study each component part in relation to the others. The bare, white canvas came close enough to giving the illusion of light foam in the sun, and its value is not much different. It demonstrates how well the bare canvas can serve until the last.

The completion of the fourth step sets the stage for the final and most critical period of all. My own habit at this time is to relax, fill my pipe, select fresh brushes and a clean rag, and replenish the pigments on my palette, all the while critically studying my sketch and the sea beyond. Heretofore, in a fever of creative energy and lightning decisions, the painting has progressed almost subconsciously. Now is the moment to appraise what has been done; to note passages that are seen at

FOURTH STEP *At this stage the rocks are painted in their general color and value as speedily as possible. Any accent of color, extraneous interest, or uncontrolled movement not compatible with this main motif is therefore eliminated or modified. The final step is demonstrated on the following page.*

once to be right, and to single out others which, for one reason or another, do not ring the bell and need further study and adjustment. The fifth and final phase becomes a matter of co-ordinating the whole into a complete expression of the pre-conceived idea or mood.

5th Step *The Final Step*

WHAT HAS BEEN accomplished in this final step is clearly shown by comparing the accompanying color plate with the preceding plate. It will be seen that the original idea, indicated in outline at the beginning, has progressed logically and without major changes to a full expression of the artist's intention. The center of interest or focal point of the picture is still the large rock in the middle foreground shown in strong relief against the unbroken white of the falling wave. The cloud, as first painted in the upper right-hand corner of the canvas, had a tendency to distract the attention from the main interest below and it has been toned down a bit. The distant water has been simplified somewhat and only a single breaking wave crest allowed to break the uniformity of its blue tonality. The forms and shapes occurring in the surging shallow water in the foreground have assumed their final placing and quantity. It is interesting to observe that they do not exactly coincide with the forms and shapes indicated earlier in the outline painting

FIFTH STEP *The completed painting.*

within that area. This was anticipated, as will be remembered.

Looking for a moment at the sweeping back surge of water in the shadow of the central rock, observe that despite all the details of foam structure and differences of color and values that have been added, the area as a whole still retains its larger movement and its shadow character.

As for the rocks, more careful and studied drawing was needed to build them up to their present form and appearance of solidity. Their rich warm color in the sun forms a strong contrast to the cool greens and purple tones of the foam waters about them. I used yellow ochre, burnt sienna, cadmium red lightest, Indian red and burnt umber in painting the rocks.

SEVEN

Moonlights

"NEVER WASTE YOUR TIME painting moonlight motifs. Their value at the most is only a sentimental one." Such, as nearly as I can remember, was the advice given to me when, as a student, I presented my first nocturnal effort to the master for criticism. Whether right or wrong, the advice went unheeded as far as I was concerned. In the twenty years intervening, I have rarely let a year go by without painting one or more moonlight subjects.

The reflection of the full moon on breaking surf has a poetic quality far removed from nature's everyday efforts. Even if painted realistically, it provokes a sense of unreality. In the turmoil of shifting patterns brought to life for fleeting moments in the path of the moon, we look into a world of abstraction. Whatever sentiment we extract from it will be what we ourselves put into it.

Upon the technical side, with which we, as painters, are concerned in our efforts to interpret its mood, it offers exceptional problems in observation and memory. Only in the summer months is it possible to paint the moon out of doors,

BLACK AND WHITE STUDY FOR MOONLIGHT

and then but for a brief hour or two. At all other times it becomes a matter of observation and memory.

I will describe my own method of collecting the necessary information for painting a moonlight picture. First I make a series of pencil sketches and notes in longhand, recording every factual observation that seems important to remember. I select a position on the rocks close to the water and make a quick sketch of my general composition. As I rarely include the moon itself in the picture, I wait until it is well above the horizon before beginning to set down my observations. I have already decided what stage of the breaking surf I want to record, as its pattern will form the basis of the picture's design. Once determined, this pattern must be adhered to in spite of all distractions. My next step is to observe and record in writing every important fact, in terms of painting, that seems vital to the task at hand. I write figure '1' in pencil at the spot or area which in nature represents the lightest light. Observing what appears to be the next lightest light, I place the figure '2' on the corresponding section of the paper, and so on down to deep black. When two or more areas, although separated, are of the same value, the same number is given to each. So far, then, I have succeeded in establishing the relative values from light to dark of each area throughout the entire sketch. Now along the margin of the paper I write numbers from one to ten or more, as may be necessary. Referring once more to nature I attempt to analyze in terms of color every pertinent fact that bears upon the area or spot designated by the figure '1' and then write that observation down against that number in the

Shorthand sketch for the painting "Silvery Rays." These penciled notes were done on the rocky shore by the light of the moon.

margin. I do this with the next lightest area marked '2' on the drawing and so on down through the numbers to the end. When finished, besides establishing all my values from light to dark, I have recorded the color relations and even the color variations of each important part of the composition, the latter described in longhand but in sufficient detail to recall it to mind for later use. This very effort to describe in words what the eye and brain have seen tends to fix the picture firmly in the memory.

LAY-IN FOR "SILVERY RAYS" *This lay-in was done in about twenty minutes. It represents the artist's conception in terms of organized simplicity. Painted in blue monotone, the color thinned with turpentine to the consistency of watercolor, it established the essentials of design and action in large areas unbroken by detail. On that foundation the painting proceeded rapidly.*

In the course of the evening, I may make several sketches and notes, each differing from the other as conditions change. But no evening thus spent is unproductive of some fresh conception for a new picture or some added bits of useful knowledge to store away. Strange to say, the following morning, when I am ready to paint and have a clear idea of the subject in mind, I refer to my notes only rarely.

Let us look across the water at the full moon in the first stages of its ascent skyward and see what happens. Our eye travels along the dazzling path of light that begins at the horizon and reflects in a direct line from the moon straight to us. Its width, when the moon is near the horizon, is the width of the moon itself, but as the moon gets higher the path broadens and spreads across the sea. We have discovered that in daylight painting the color of the sea depends upon condi-

SILVERY RAYS *(25 x 30)*

tions in the sky, particularly upon the position of the sun. In moonlight, we look for the same interrelation of all the elements and we note that the colors of the sea and sky and rocks depend upon the position of the moon, atmospheric influences, and the presence of clouds in the night sky.

For the purpose of demonstration, let us establish an arbitrary moonlight condition and see if we cannot discover certain fundamental facts that will be useful to us at all times. We shall assume the moon to be an hour or two above the horizon and our center of interest, the surf in front of us. If we look in the direction of the moon, the path of its reflection is directly in line with our vision. Our lightest value will be the sparkles occurring in the unbroken black water in the moon's path; they are as brilliant as the moon itself. Naturally they have less intensity in the distance. The sea is usually darker than the sky, and all forms and shapes become less well defined in proportion to their distance from the moon path.

Whenever a wave or body of foam is seen against the path of light behind, it appears as a dark silhouette.

When the wave is solid water, it is our darkest value. When a wave breaks and fills the foreground with foam it naturally reflects the color and light of the moon, but because the texture of this foam is not so smooth as unbroken water, it absorbs more light and consequently reflects less. The result is that, even in the direct path of light, this broken foam area nowhere approaches the intense brightness of the sparkles. And the large area of broken surf which sometimes extends on either side of the moon path tends towards a dull flat white. Therefore, it can be said that the lightest light and the darkest dark are in the direct path of the moon, and that all outside is lower in key and less well defined in form.

When we come to painting the rocks in our moonlight picture, we truly have a problem. To say that they seem almost black in the shadow parts, or when silhouetted against the light, is quite true but not very helpful. Assuming black to be the absence of light, then our rocks are indeed dark but not black; many influences modify both their value and color.

There is a velvety quality in their seeming blackness that is difficult to achieve in paint. They appear neither wholly warm in tone nor cool; paradoxically they seem to be both. Cer-

HARVEST MOON *(24 x 42) Here for the first time the moon itself appears in the picture. In all other examples shown, we have been interested only in the moon's reflection on the water. The inclusion of both the moon and its reflection presents a problem of divided interests which must be solved to insure a focal unity. The higher the moon above the horizon, the more difficult it is to combine satisfactorily the two in the same painting. In "Harvest Moon," I have deliberately toned down the light intensity of the moon disc, and lightened the sky area surrounding it, in order to lessen its contrast with the sky. Notice that the dry sand is quite dark in value and does not reflect the light from the moon. Notice again how the concentric wave-ripples in the foreground foam area are outlined by their shadow markings.*

Courtesy of Doll & Richards Gallery

THE LIFE BOAT *(25 x 30) A trip to Bermuda supplied the inspiration for this picture. Sitting on the top deck at night, watching the ship's rigging sway back and forth against the brilliant light of a full moon, suggested the possibility of an unusual design. However, the first idea of topmast and stays was discarded, the lifeboat seeming to afford greater interest, particularly as the lower viewpoint offered better opportunity for painting the sea itself.*

tainly, their darkness has life and vibrancy. A simple experiment will show what I mean. Select an area of rock in your painting that you intend to be one of your darkest values. Paint it as you would normally with your dark pigments—say, burnt umber, ultramarine deep, and perhaps a bit of deep red and mars violet. When finished, you have probably succeeded in attaining the proper dark value but you find that it lacks depth and tends to be dull and opaque. Now take your palette knife and scrape the painted area with the thin long edge, removing the superfluous paint. What remains on the canvas will still give forth the dark value of the rock, but, owing to the texture of the linen, you will note that the scraped surface has assumed a vibrant quality. Just how much you may have to add to or modify the scraped area depends on its relation to the rest of your painting.

These dark rocks in the moonlight present much the same

BASS ROCKS, MOONLIGHT *(24 x 30). Here is an attempt to show the light of the moon breaking through the clouds and casting a brilliant path on the sea, culminating in the dramatic action on the shore. This painting seems to suggest a poetic and emotional approach by the artist. Laying aside (for the moment) the technical aspects involved, a certain measure of these qualities must be present if one is to reveal the total impact of moonlight on moving waters. To the layman it is a thrilling sight; to the painter, it is that and more, for he has to interpret his reaction from his knowledge and memory, and then reveal his interpretation to others. Only constant observation over the years can supply that knowledge. Private Collection.*

difficulties as do shadow areas in daylight pictures. The very fact that both are neutral in tone asserts that they are not a color which is easy to remember, to be brought out on any suitable occasion. Every condition of light has its corresponding neutrals; so it follows that in moonlight the color and value of these rocks in the shadow parts will be determined by the quality of the moonlight and will differ in every picture.

We begin with certain premises of light conditions and the rest follows logically. As painters, we are not interested in a single color nor do we attempt to isolate it; we deal only with color relations. From my own experience of painting moon-

IN THE PATH OF THE MOON *(25 x 30) This canvas was painted the following morning from pencil notes made one night at York, Maine. The little spot of light on the horizon, to the right of the moon path, represents Nubble Light. In contrast to the painting called "Moonlight Ogunquit," it will be seen that here the moon has but recently risen, and makes only a narrow light path on the water. Observe that the wave breaking in the center of the picture is as dark in value as the rock below it. Both are in the moon path and on a plane directly opposite the source of light. The lightest lights are the sparkles in the smooth water this side of the foreground rock and in the pools of water on the top surface of the rock.*

Courtesy of Joseph Skinner collection, Holyoke, Mass.

Courtesy of Mrs. Luke Wilson, Washington, D.C.

MOONLIGHT, OGUNQUIT *(25 x 30) "Moonlight Ogunquit" illustrates the effect on the water when the clear light of a full moon shines down upon it from almost overhead. From its high position in the heavens, the moon fairly floods the sea and shore with its cold white light. Compare this picture with "Harvest Moon" and note what totally different moods they express. This difference emphasizes the truth that the quality of moonlight is no more the same at all times than is the quality of the light from the sun from dawn to dusk.*

lights, I am more than ever convinced that the successful moonlight picture is one that conveys feeling and mood, rather than realism or cleverness in handling. Even the basic color scheme is unimportant if the illusion is convincing. By that I mean that it makes little difference if blue, brown or green is the prevailing color scheme—I have seen good examples of all three. What really counts is the mood which the artist projects by his own personal interpretation of the subject.

It is unfortunate that nature offers the painter of moonlight subjects so few opportunities to study the effects he is eager to dramatize in his pictures. Ideal conditions for such studies would be, of course, heavy surf, full or nearly full moon, and clear visibility. How seldom all of these conditions occur simultaneously may be gathered from a record I kept for the five months from May to September, 1946, on Cape Ann. Never during the full moon period in those months did all three conditions prevail at the same time. There were many beautiful nights under a full moon but, alas, no surf. One moonlight period offered a fair amount of sea action but clouds continually obscured the moon.

Nature sometimes is chary of her finest moments. Once, years ago in Ogunquit, my patience was rewarded with a truly supreme example of what can happen when, under a full moon, tremendous seas break upon a rocky shore. The memory of it has colored and affected, and in part inspired, the painting of every moonlight of mine ever since. The possibility of witnessing another such spectacle has kept me always on the alert whenever the moon is full. We paint well only what we feel strongly, and moonlights are no exception.

EIGHT

The Hurricane

THE ARTIST, in New England particularly, learns to take nothing for granted, not even the weather. So perhaps it may be appropriate here to caution those eager and fearless painters who have not lived their lives within sight of the ocean long enough to learn how fickle the weather—consequently the sea—can be, and how necessary it is to be wary when painting on a rocky shore. "Familiarity breeds contempt," the saying goes, but sooner or later those who spend much time on the seacoast acquire a familiarity with the ocean which certainly induces respect. The novice sees no menace in the gentle waves that break upon the point and harmlessly sweep inland through the cleft rocks. He dashes madly seaward for a closer view. In due time comes the big wave. With little warning, it sweeps in, far and beyond any point hitherto reached, and with it goes the innocence of the uninitiated.

It seems impossible that the peaceful and placid ocean of a calm summer's day can be aroused to such tragic fury as it was one afternoon of a day in September, 1938 that began like any other pleasant autumn day. By chance, I was painting that afternoon on Halibut Point, a few miles above Rockport on

AFTER THE HURRICANE *(30 x 36) The onrushing movement of the sea is the paramount interest in this picture. A continuous succession of waves pile into the cove with cumulative power, one almost on top of the other. A gray tonality envelops the whole. It is a frank expression of realism in marine painting.*

Cape Ann. Seated on the rocks with my sketch box and my half-finished sketch in front of me, I became aware that the wind had freshened considerably and was blowing from the southeast, which is rather unusual in that locality. I noticed, too, that the air was extremely warm and humid. I went on with my sketch but soon was unable to keep the paint box with its upraised lid steady upon the rock. I finally gave up and started to walk home with the wind in my face. The road skirted the shore. As I looked seaward I could hardly believe what was taking place before my eyes. The waves were making up with unaccustomed suddenness. Although as yet visibility was good and the sky was not all overcast, it was filled with scattered dark clouds racing at tremendous speed against a queer yellowish background. The wind was increasing with every step I took, and by the time I reached home it was approaching gale force. There was no doubt that something serious was brewing, although not in the memory of anyone living had a hurricane ever reached New England. I got my car, gathered some friends and drove down to Straitsmouth Cove. It was now impossible to stand before the full force of the wind, but, getting somewhat in the lee of a house, we secured a vantage point from which it was possible to look out to sea beyond the Cove. It was raining by now, not in a steady downpour but in spotty gusts. The whole scene was charged with motion. Wave after wave swept in to shore, one succeeding another with terrific rapidity and, as they pounded in, they crowded upon each other in endless succession. As each wave rose to break, the wind behind blew the foam and spume from the crests in a parallel line hundreds of yards towards the shore. The noise of the wind and the crash of the breakers were deafening. Changed beyond recognition was the peaceful cove of a short time ago. It was dramatic, it was appalling, but the heart of a marine painter could not but thrill at the spectacle.

There was, of course, no opportunity to sketch under such conditions. Yet, even as I stood there, a picture was forming in my mind and subconsciously I was noting certain details of color and form and strange effects of wind that distinguished this storm from all others. This time, at least, I would have only my memory of the vital and important aspects of the storm to serve me.

Darkness had fallen before we left the Cove; yet even those few hours had left their mark upon the streets of the little town. We picked our way by the light of automobile lamps through a welter of strewn branches, here and there noting great elms that had fallen before the wind, one, in particular, leaning against the demolished roof of a small frame dwelling.

STORM AT SEA *(34 x 40) This canvas attempts to show the awful grandeur of a storm at sea. The interest of the picture has been focused upon the crest of a wave which is seen in silhouette against the clearing sky. The vertical downward movement of the rain at the left provides a natural contrast to the many horizontal lines of the ocean, and at the same time helps to confine the area of special interest. It will be observed that, although most of the strongest structural lines of the waves are horizontal, various means have been employed to direct the eye in a counter direction and toward the focal point.*

The hurricane of 1938 is now history and would not be mentioned here except to point out that anything unusual in the matter of weather is possible in New England and that, although the marine painter cannot often hope to have an orchestra seat at such a performance, he must always be on the alert for the unexpected and the spectacular.

The next morning I stretched a fairly large canvas and attempted to record my own impression of what I had seen. The picture was named "After the Hurricane."

NINE

Skies

THE MORE FAMILIAR we become with the moods and aspects of the ocean, the more we realize how predominantly a part of the ever changing drama is the sky that gives it light and color. And the more intently do we study it under the many varying conditions that account for its surprising and beautiful effects.

An entire book might well be devoted to the sky and the fascinating architecture of clouds. But, of course, the painter has to acquire his knowledge through direct and persistent observation of nature. That knowledge cannot be too complete. It should embrace not only what the heavens themselves look like, but how they are likely to appear when the sea is putting on a particular kind of show. Whatever the show, the sky plays a leading, if not the stellar, role. In my "Storm at Sea" (p. 76), for example, the tempestuous clouds supply the major dramatic note for the entire painting. In some pictures, as in the demonstration subject on page 59, the sky, occupying a relatively small area of the canvas, is less important in the all-over effect. Yet it should be related in mood, in movement, and color to the water if the picture is to hold together as a unified expression.

That relationship is pretty obvious when we consider that both ocean and sky are conditioned by the same weather. A stiff blow that accents the sea with white caps also does something to the forms and movements of clouds. We note that the sea takes on a bright cobalt or ultramarine hue when the sky is a clear, brilliant blue. Those who have painted around the Gulf of Mexico know that the more brilliant skies of the tropics touch the waters with quite a different and more intense kind of blue than is seen in northern latitudes. When fog or squalls draw a gray curtain over the sky, the ocean responds with leaden hues.

The beginner impressed by the brilliant blue of a summer

EASTERLY BLOW *(24 x 40) Marine subjects lend themselves readily to overmantel dimensions. Although many interests are embraced in the picture as a whole, the main emphasis has been concentrated on the burst of spray in the center. Throwing the near foreground in the shadow helps in directing attention to this focal point.*

sky can easily be deceived by its subtle quality. That blue can never be simulated by a mixture of pure pigment from the tube mixed with white. It always is modified with yellow, red or purple—or all three. Even though the student, with untrained eye, cannot detect the presence of these delicate hues, he should experiment with such modifications of his blues. The results will be convincing and will develop his powers of observation.

Whether painting the sea or the land, we must realize that the colors of the sky at the horizon and overhead are never the same. Over the land there is a film of dust and smoke. The density of this film and its depth vary according to conditions on earth. In industrial areas it is very heavy; in the open country the atmosphere is clear and the dust film is thin. But always there is some degree of film through which the colors of the sky are seen. Looking upward, our vision need penetrate only the depth of this dusty veil; but looking toward the horizon, the whole vast extent of the veil lying along the earth's surface separates us from the blue. This dense film either grays the sky color or, under certain conditions, reflects the sun's rays in such manner as to produce a variety of hues, sometimes quite brilliant.

Over the open ocean the smoke and dust of the land is quickly dispelled. In its place is a film of vapor which acts in a similar way to condition distant sky colors at the horizon. So it is that the sky at the horizon is seldom very blue. On an ordinary clear day, when there are no clouds, we observe many gradations in color from horizon to zenith. Starting at the horizon with cool pink and lavender, the sequence might be through orange, yellow, yellow-green, green-blue, and cobalt, to cobalt deep overhead.

The particles of the atmospheric veil, as I have said, sometimes reflect many colors from the sun. This is particularly true of the moisture film that overlays the ocean. It is not strange, then, that the color of the sky at the horizon often takes on surprising hues.

PUTTING IN *(30 x 36) A dramatic pictorial version of "man against the sea." This solitary human being, pitting his frail energy against nature's mighty forces, is a symbol that has been used time and again, notably by Millet in "The Sower" and Homer in "Fog Warning." The author's student days were spent in many of New England's coastal towns and the lobsterman at his calling provided similar subjects, the inspiration for many of his canvases.*

A sunless sky may be a warm gray or a cool gray, and these grays are very subtle. With experience one learns to detect the color mixtures that produce particular effects. Whenever possible, study Winslow Homer's skies. These, although on the gray side, are seldom alike.

It goes without saying that the study of the work of any painter is helpful, along with direct observation of the sky itself. And if you cannot see the original canvases, reproductions will serve, even though they may not be in color. If the reproductions are in halftone, they will at least demonstrate values and composition, especially the latter. Observe how the marine painter designs his sky as a back drop for the sea. If I may point to my "Storm at Sea" again, note the way I used the half circle of light in the threatening sky to focus upon the bit of white surf on the crest of a wave that becomes the center of interest in the canvas. Note also how the small light spots—breaks in the dark clouds—complement the light surf areas below.

By way of contrast, turn to the reproduction of "Straits-

THE CHALLENGE *(30 x 40) The design of this picture is exceedingly simple. The surf is sharply silhouetted against a very dark sky and sea which unite in creating a dramatic foil for the light, foaming waters. Emphasis is thus focused principally upon this aspect of the stirring scene.*

mouth Light" on page 32. Here the sky shows no pronounced pattern of light and dark, but is in violent movement, the clouds scudding before the offshore breeze that is piling up the surf on the rocks.

How different is "Easterly Blow" (p. 78)! Here the sky is clear and the cumulus clouds repeat the surf forms. Note how sky and ocean are tied together by the big surf mass which silhouettes like a cloud against the sky.

Now turn to page 103 and study Frederick Waugh's "Wild Weather." The lines of the sea and surf are horizontal, stretching across the canvas. The clouds, likewise horizontal, are wholly in harmony with this lateral movement.

In "The Challenge," the sky, merging with the distant sea—as it often does—is dark and relatively flat in value. I planned this in order to give the great burst of surf its most dramatic silhouette effect. I studied those two cloud masses very carefully. They play an important, though minor, role in the picture. They had to be low in value, avoiding competition with the foreground surf, yet the picture certainly would be weakened without them.

I have urged the beginner to be thorough in his study of the sky under all conditions of light, wind, and weather. It is obvious, I am sure, that this is essential to the vocabulary of the marine painter. Some painters have made the mistake of repeating a successful formula in picture after picture, having learned how to paint a particular kind of sky. Thus they have been identified with that formula, have grown famous for it. They become slaves to their own invention and to the demand by dealers to continue to produce the kind of picture the public has become accustomed to expect from their brush.

I have found that the sky and clouds are at their best in mid-morning and from mid-afternoon to evening. These are the best periods for all outdoor painting. Least interesting are the hours when the sun is high in the heavens and beats all color out of the scene below. In the late afternoon, shadows lengthen, clouds accumulate, and the sea takes on a richer hue.

When beginning to paint the sky, I lay it in—the entire area—as rapidly as possible, leaving until later its modification by broken color and clouds, which depend so entirely upon what goes on in the sea itself. But everyone works differently and the instructor can only advise what he, in his experience, has found most useful to his own purpose.

TEN

Rocks

THE SERIOUS STUDENT of marine painting spends a good deal of time studying the anatomy and color of rocks. Rocks often occupy as much as, or even more than, the area taken up in the canvas by waves and surf. Always, they are a determining factor in the picture's success. No surf, however well painted, can be convincing if it is required to dash against papier mache rocks.

Geological formation varies at different places on the coast line, and the character of rocks is modified by the impact the sea has had upon them. Some rocks of stratified structure are readily broken down by the pounding of the sea and are constantly presenting fresh, flat, sharp-edged planes that catch the light and produce striking patterns. Others, harder and not stratified, are worn smooth and rounded. There are rocks which break up or wear into grotesque shapes; these are too freakish to be useful in the average picture.

At the beginning of a surf painting we have to decide how the rocks are to be treated. Shall they be principally in silhouette, or do we want to take advantage of the light and shadow pattern that is seen when the sun is full upon them?

Suppose we take a look at a number of pictures and note how that question was variously answered.

In "The Challenge" (p. 81) we see the rocks chiefly as dark masses. Their structure has been so fully subordinated to the surf that we are scarcely conscious of their forms, certainly not of their individuality. Here, rocks and sky, all very dark, combine to produce a dark background against which the surf pattern stands out in sharply defined silhouette. How ill-advised it would have been to have broken up that solid rock mass as was done in "The Green Cove."

Note in "The Green Cove" how the sunlight playing upon the stratified rock planes has created interesting pattern—and, of course, color. The rocks of "The Challenge" would have been out of place here.

THE GREEN COVE *(24 x 32) "The Green Cove," painted on the Maine coast near York Cliffs, shows how rugged rock contours can be utilized as a main motif in a picture. Notice how the afternoon sun from the right illumines all rock surfaces facing it directly, throwing all else into shadow. Yet even those surface planes away from the direct light are not uniform in color or value as many of them, especially if broad and flat, reflect a light, cool tone from the blue sky to the left.*

In "Easterly Blow" (p. 78) the rocks are used chiefly for silhouette value, but there is considerable definition of structure and the rocks are interesting in themselves. However, comparing them with the "Green Cove" rocks, it will be seen that quite a different handling was indicated for each picture. It is always revealing to make such comparisons; to imagine how a given canvas would look if the rocks of another subject were substituted. That exercise makes us realize how greatly we need to know our rocks and to appreciate their possibilities under varying conditions. It is interesting, for example, to look from "The Challenge" to "Straitsmouth Light" (p. 32). In both pictures the rocks are partly merged, in tone, with the waves, so that we are less conscious of them than in the former, where the white surf brings them into sharp relief.

Now in "Briar Neck Surf" (p. 48) the rocks vie with the surf for our attention. They monopolize the foreground, and we feel their great solidity and weight. Their structure is clearly defined but—and this is important here—the light and shadow treatment does not break up the contour of their dark mass. Note also that rocks and distant water are about the same value. Together they serve as a foil for the white surf which is sharply cut out against them, except for the dashing spray at the extreme left.

The rocks in "Moonlight, Ogunquit" (p. 71) are treated still differently. As in "The Challenge," they appear principally as dark mass, their individual forms being scarcely defined. However, the brilliant moonlight, illuminating their flat tops, does give them a strong three-dimensional feeling. It is clear that they are outcroppings from a horizontal shelf that is nearly covered by the swirling foam. Note the horizontal emphasis in the rock mass, harmonizing with the horizon line, which is unbroken except for the slight bit of spray that barely cuts across it.

One way to overcome the tendency to paint rocks as though they were made of papier mache is to underpaint them first in a warm dark tone, building up later to the proper color and value. Avoid paying too much attention to reflected light in

Courtesy of Leonard Raymond, York Harbor, Maine

APRIL SEA *(30 x 36) This is an attempt to interpret the type of day that comes frequently in the spring of the year to Cape Ann. The wind is northwest and the air is cool and clear after the easterly storm of the day before. The sea is blue and a fairly heavy surf is still boiling among the rocks. The shape or pattern of the broken formations is clearly defined against the deep blue and green of smoother water and becomes an important feature in the picture design. The rocks standing in strong sunlight are painted in simple light and shade, and not much attempt is made to look into the shadow parts for reflected light.*

the shadows. This breaks up the simplicity of the essential shadow pattern which should be a simple statement of structural fact instead of a catalog of incidental happenings.

Rocks are as varied in color as they are in formation, and of course their colors are modified when the waves varnish them with a wet film and when a setting sun gilds them for a brief moment. When the local color is light ochre or orange-red, brilliance conferred by the setting sun is astonishing indeed. The sun falling upon the rocks, at any time of day, produces a great variety of shades and tints of the prevailing local color, due to the different angles the various planes present to the source of light. This is well illustrated in "April Sea," reproduced on page 87.

In the preceding chapter, we dwelt at considerable length on the influences of the sky upon the color of the ocean. We stressed the point that both of these elements complement each other, producing a harmonious ensemble. The rocks must, of course, play a cooperative part in this ensemble. Local color in rocks influences the color of the adjacent water. Light, reflected up into rock shadows by the moving water, still further pulls both together in color compatibility. Sky, water, surf, rocks—all are instruments in the achievement of a single theme. We must never forget this singleness of purpose, the absolute need for interplay of color throughout the entire picture.

ELEVEN

Where to Paint

THE OCEAN is the ocean wherever you find it! So the untraveled might reason, but those who have sailed the seven seas, particularly artists, know that the oceans of the tropics and those of the north temperate zones have somewhat different characteristics. To paint the sea in new climes and on foreign shores is a broadening experience. It challenges the painter's skill and it stimulates him, especially when his work is in danger of getting stale.

Brought up on the New England coast and familiar with its gray-green waters, its fogs, and the dark blue, quiet seas of the summer months, I was unprepared for the lavish display of color I found when first I painted in the tropics. It was at once a revelation and an experience. My palette underwent a pronounced change. It had to, in order to cope with the quite different array of brilliant hues. There were no rocks, of course, but white sand and palm trees took their place as elements in the composition.

The comparatively short space of shore line between Ogunquit Beach, Maine, on the north and York Beach to the south boasts the most paintable stretch of rocky coast and inlets to be found on our American shores. Where else is there contained, in so limited an area, a coast line as rugged and varied and at the same time so accessible to the painter? Some other familiar shores have odd and grotesque rock formations which, when painted, draw more attention to the locale of the picture as a "point of interest" than to the eternal conflict of sea and shore. Such is not the character of the New England coast. It is rugged and dramatic, but it is not so startlingly "scenic" as to steal the show from the valid qualities of a good marine

ROCKY NECK, GLOUCESTER *(25 x 30) One day I was looking about for a subject to paint among the wharves of Gloucester, and seeking something different from the usual viewpoint. Quickly climbing the hill overlooking the city, I looked down upon a maze of boats, masts, docks, fish factories; and far in the distance upon the outer harbor and hills. The fresh outlook stimulated my interest, and with great enthusiasm I painted and completed the below 25" x 30" canvas. It was a gray day, the kind that rains intermittently. Rocky Neck, in the middle distance, is composed of mostly red buildings with an occasional white one. The factory in the foreground is a dull yellow. It will be seen how the smoke from the chimney on the left ties together the foreground and the middle distance, and the tall sail just to the right foreground does the same for the far distance.*

Courtesy of Addison Gilbert Hospital, Gloucester, Mass.

painting. The professional painter is not interested in making a portrait of a particular scene; his purpose is to record the drama of sea and shore as it may be observed the world over where conditions favor its best performance.

By a close and realistic study of the particular, we arrive paradoxically at the general. Our rocks and sea, having no localized or identifying feature, become a symbol of all rocks and sea. Each person who studies such a painting reads into it his own experience as revealed to him through the skill of the artist.

The color of the Ogunquit rocks varies considerably; some are gray and rather neutral in tone while others tend toward ochre and dark red. At Ogunquit itself there is a river with a wide estuary at its mouth and with sand dunes extending for miles up the beach toward Kennebunk. For years my studio overlooking the beach was an ideal spot to study waves rolling in unchecked over level sands. Marine painters like Alexander Harrison attained fame in painting this one type of seascape.

Cape Ann, Massachusetts, is geologically composed almost entirely of granite, and along its shores the rocky headlands generally have the color of light ochre and orange-red. This can become monotonous if painted too often. "April Sea" (page 87) gives a rough idea of their color tonality. Otherwise, from Bass Rocks, East Gloucester, north to Andrews Point beyond Pigeon Cove, Cape Ann holds much of interest for the marine painter.

Monhegan Island off the coast of Maine has long been the mecca of sea painters. George Bellows maintained a studio there and Eric Hudson painted some of his best marines from its shores. Its tendency to be fog-ridden much of the time proved too depressing for my temperament, and I rarely paint there now. However, I recognize that in its dramatic isolation, it can be an inspiration to the right painter. The same can be said for the island of Grand Manan farther to the north.

One has to travel the California coast to Point Lobos, Carmel, and Monterey to find a few miles of Pacific coast line that is made to order for the marine painter. William Ritschel has shown the world some of its potentialities. In addition to its rugged rocks, its shores are dotted with graceful cypress trees which, in conjunction with the ocean background, constitute a decorative motif not to be found elsewhere on the American coast lines.

I have painted on the Oregon and Washington shores and along the Juan de Fuca Straits opposite Vancouver Island. I was greatly impressed with the giant monolithic boulders that lie there, scattered offshore, and appreciated their possibilities in marine composition, but their interest seemed to me as much geological as artistic. The immense shore line confining these two states has few rocky harbors or inlets, and often the high bluffs, covered with Douglas fir, meet the ocean directly—not a favorable situation for the marine painter.

My favorite spots in southern waters are the west coast of Florida near Sarasota, where the Gulf of Mexico seems particularly brilliant as seen through the palm trees of Siesta and Long Boat Keys, and on the island of Puerto Rico, not a great distance from San Juan. Whenever I have been there the steady trade winds were a source of continuous, heavy surf. The breakers formed and broke far out to sea, a phenomenon not common to the deeper water of our New England coast. See my picture, "Where the Trade Winds Blow" (p. 93).

In Bermuda the island waters have all the familiar colors of the true tropics. But the rock-like formations of coral or limestone are eroded and pitted by the action of the sea into odd and curious shapes, and seem to lack the dignity necessary for the marine motif. I found it more satisfying to work in watercolor in Bermuda in my attempts to render the brilliant contrasts which are so characteristic of that locality.

Nassau waters are particularly brilliant, dazzling almost, but as I was there after one of the big hurricanes which had devastated the protective trees, I found little shelter from the sun, and the most satisfying subjects to paint seemed to be the innumerable sponge boats at the quay, crowded to the gunwales with native fisher folk and livestock.

There is a spot in England off the coast of Cornwall where

Courtesy of Leonard Raymond, York Harbor, Maine

WHERE THE TRADE WINDS BLOW *(32 x 44) This picture was painted in Puerto Rico. Instead of rocks and cliffs, a group of palm trees provides the opposing elements to the inrushing sea. Note how the small palmetto at the right, by the importance of lone position, balances the clump of palms on the left.*

The most striking color characteristic is the strong contrast between the warm orange and reds of the shore area and the cool blues and emerald green and white of the sea. To aid in getting this contrast, I first underpainted the ground area and trees with a thin stain of raw and burnt sienna diluted with turpentine. This was not done to the rest of the canvas.

On these windward shores of Puerto Rico the waves break far out to sea and then again close into shore.

I had need of my entire palette of eighteen pigments to do justice to the lavishness of tropical color.

many of the great marine painters have recorded the age-old drama of sea and shore. Paul Dougherty painted there. Homer visited it and later in his studio at Prout's Neck, Maine, painted several important canvases from sketches made upon its shores. Its dominant characteristic is the great cliffs which rise from the beaches and fishing villages at their feet. I saw them once from a ship during World War I, and it is my hope some day to return and paint them. We have nothing quite like these towering cliffs on our side of the Atlantic. It is true that on the ocean side of Monhegan Island there are two great rock promontories, called, I believe, Whitehead and Blackhead, but for my part I was never able to get interested in them as subjects for painting. Around the Gaspé Peninsula in Canada, there are some interesting sea and cliff motifs which have attracted many painters.

And lastly we come to what might be called "open sea painting." Here there is no other course for the marine student than to sail, if not the seven seas, at least as many of them as

THE DORYMAN *(16 x 20) In winter and summer, in storm or quiet, this Marblehead lobsterman visits his traps along the Coast. In his power dory, long since superseding the rowboat, he plows ahead, often through heavy seas. This 16" x 20" sketch attempts to convey the spirit of his venturesome calling. He controls the rudder of his craft with a stick attached to ropes which run through pulleys lengthwise to the vessel. With great skill he steers close to the shining buoy bearing his own painted color design and, reaching over with hooked stick, catches the loose rope attached to the buoy and hauls it aboard. Shutting off the motor, he hauls, hand over hand, on the rope attached to the trap and, from the floor of the ocen bed, brings the driping lobster pot to light.*

Courtesy of Dr. Carl W. Walter, Boston, Mass.

THE WRECK OF THE "WILKIE DAWN" *(28 x 36) Sometime after this picture was painted and exhibited the canvas once more found itself back in my studio. Looking at it with a fresh eye after the lapse of several years it seemed to me that the large white foam area in the foreground looked empty, so I painted a half submerged spar in the lower lefthand corner pointing diagonally in the direction of the ship's stern. The broken spar is now an integral part of the picture as it is today and adds immeasurably to the strength of the composition.*

he can. In these days of easy ocean travel it is a simple matter to arrange an ocean trip, even if it be only a coastwise voyage, say from New York to New Orleans, a trip I have taken many times. Nothing but ocean and sky for days and nights on end. What more is necessary for the marine painter? The whole mightiness of the sea is all about him. Even if his sketches seem hopelessly inadequate, the important thing is to paint, observe, and memorize. The sketch is the tangible thing that you bring back with you; in your mind and memory are the intangible emotions which, after all, supply the inspiration for any pictures that come out of your travel experiences. These, lying dormant, are later recalled by one or more of the sketches made on shipboard when, in your studio, you take up your brush to paint a canvas of the open sea.

TWELVE

Gallery of Marine Paintings

In the following group of new illustrations for the revised and enlarged edition of Marine Painting, *I have tried to choose those paintings whose subject matter and color differences would present to the student various aspects of the sea. Among them are examples of the ocean at night in moonlight; rocks and surf in sunlight, under grey skies, and under stormy skies. In some, the sea is in violent motion; in one picture at least, a dead calm prevails; in a few instances figures are included. In short, among these paintings can be found a cross section of the infinite variety of motifs associated with marine painting.*

For those who would paint the sea, there is no substitute for the daily sketch in oils out-of-doors, observing and recording conditions as they appear at the time. Sketches will provide a growing library for future reference in the years to come. All of the paintings on the following pages are based on the experience gained in this fashion; in many cases, the painting is but the fulfillment of the quick, yet careful, study in the open air.

I believe that art is related to nature and to the life around us; the true expression of the artist's personality is revealed in his reaction to each, in terms of realism and imagination combined with disciplined craftsmanship.

THE POWER AND THE GLORY, *oil, 30 x 40.* The majesty and awesomeness of the ocean are best appreciated, perhaps, from the viewpoint of a small boat in the open sea. Thus seen, the mountainous waves crest high against the sky, at times seeming to shut out all else from view. The great forces involved are elemental, and the artist must first choose the most important structural lines to convey the great sweep of action. Without *opposition*, no sense of motion can be conveyed; the astronaut in a vacuum, with no guideposts, travelling at 18,000 miles an hour, may *appear* relatively motionless. In this painting, it is easy to distinguish the opposing areas of movement, which create the action. There are details, of course, but they are always only a part of some larger unit. Note how the narrow skyline tends to magnify the height and bigness of the great wave.

WINTER SEA, *oil, 30 x 36.* If you wish to convey strength, dignity, and power, as one often does in a marine painting, it is well to have simplicity of design in a well-defined pattern. A test would be: does the picture look almost as good in black and white as in color. I believe this painting succeeds when viewed with that question in mind. All the dark and light elements are large and bold in form: the clouds, the distant sea, the black rocks, the white foam, and the crashing wave. There is no timidity or indecision in the ocean on such a day, and there should be none in the painting. This type of painting, if reduced photographically to postage stamp size, would still retain clearly the elemental structure of the original composition. *Collection, Dr. Clyde Woodworth, Beverly, Massachusetts.*

PATH OF GOLD, *oil, 38 x 44*. The artist has countless ways to dramatize his subject, none more effective, perhaps, than the device of the silhouette. In this painting, two things have been done to heighten the effect. Not only has the most interesting feature of the ship been thrown into strongest relief, but, for added effect, the ship is seen at night against the light of a golden moon. The eye takes in the path of the moon on the water, the figure on the bowsprit, and only afterwards is one aware of the huge hull and intricate rigging, subdued but fully recorded. The picture is frankly an imaginative glimpse into the romantic past. The general color scheme is green and yellow. *Awarded Richard Mitton Memorial Gold Medal, Jordan Marsh 30th Annual Exhibition, 1965.*

THE CHASM AT NIGHT, *oil, 30 x 36.* Moonlight on the seacoast casts a magic spell over most people. In this painting, the eye follows the moon's ever-brightening path from the far horizon to the rocky shore in the foreground. The light finds its way up every nook and cranny, and sparkles and glitters on the wet rocks on either side of the great crevice. Perhaps the painting's most interesting feature is the reflected glow on the smooth inner walls of the cleft, telling us that there is plenty of white boiling water far below, reflecting the direct moonlight into the chasm. Moonlight should be felt; its charm and mysterious beauty must be recognized and met halfway by the painter. It should not be considered entirely a problem in abstraction. *Private Collection.*

WRECK OFF EASTERN POINT, *oil, 20 x 24.* Several years ago, we on Cape Ann heard over the radio that a Gloucester dragger had been wrecked during the night off Eastern Point. Next morning, many of us were on the spot. By that time, the Captain and small crew were safe on the shore, watching two thieves at work stealing the valuable navigating instruments. Finally, a policeman arrived, but could do nothing while the men remained on the wrecked craft. At last, the law officer left the scene to telephone for help from a house a half mile away. The law breakers promptly left the vessel, swam ashore, ran to their hidden car, and vanished with their loot. This painting is an attempt to record the event. *Private Collection.*

SURF OFF HALIBUT POINT, *oil, 25 x 30.* Certain aspects of changing weather conditions sometimes combine to afford an unusual or dramatic effect. This painting was due to a happy coincidence; I was in the right spot at the right time, when a passing storm dissipated over the horizon in the late afternoon, as the sun was about to set in the west. The combination of the two events brought into splendid contrast the cool, blue-green and purple sea, and the warm orange-pink of the sun-tipped clouds. Halibut Point off Cape Ann is one of our easternmost land areas in the Atlantic. Whenever the sea is running, there is certain to be splendid surf hitting these shores, often when surf can be found nowhere else. *Collection, Dr. Clyde Woodworth, Beverly, Massachusetts.*

ALONG THE COAST, *oil, 32 x 44.* Ordinarily, I like to get down low among the rocks, where the action is all about me; but in this instance I adopted a more distant view of the sea and cliffs. It is a large canvas, appropriate to this type of composition. It is well to come to the scene of action with a free mind and to let decisions about the form of the picture be dictated by the prevailing conditions of the moment. Factors to be considered might be the tide—coming in or going out? high or low?—direction of the light, time of day, degree of surf running, general disposition of rock formations and land areas, etc. Each has a bearing on the final go-ahead. But once you have determined a plan of action, stay with it to the end. I have found, to my sorrow, that it is fatal to attempt to paint two pictures at the same time on one canvas. *Courtesy, Clara De Windt, Newburyport, Massachusetts.*

MOONLIGHT ON THE MAINE COAST, *oil, 24 x 30.* In this painting, the moon is riding high and consequently out of sight, but it floods the bay with light almost from end to end. The land in the distance is slightly darker than the sky, with the lights in the houses clearly visible. The brilliance of the lighthouse beam is scarcely dimmed by the brightness of the moon overhead, an observation that amazed me at the time. I suspect that part of the reason is that the beacon light was warm yellow in tone, in contrast to the cold, silvery white of the moon above. A point to remember: were the moon lower down towards the horizon, and the eye level the same, the value of the spray thrown back from the rock in the foreground would be darker. *Collection, Miss Bette Davis, Beverly Hills, California.*

THE OLD DROGHER, *oil, 24 x 30.* I caught this action of the old coastal lumber schooner, about to let down sail, off the island of Grand Manan, situated off the coast of northern Maine. The picture was painted with a palette knife on a Masonite panel, which I had previously prepared in the usual manner, described earlier in the book. There is no doubt that painting with the palette knife produces effects unattainable with the brush. Some painters have found the method so much to their liking that they have continued doing so, and have built their careers on palette knife painting. I have spoken elsewhere of the strength and force which the employment of a silhouette gives to the design of a painting. "The Old Drogher" is a prime example of this device. *Courtesy, Mrs. Edward Smith, Darien, Connecticut.*

BLUE HORIZON, *oil, 25 x 30.* I believe that painting a marine in sunlight is more difficult than painting one with an overcast sky in a few low key colors. In the first instance, the entire range of color—from warm yellow to cold blue—exists, and values vary from very light to very dark. The color in the rocks varies from warm, light red in the sun to cold, dark purple in the shadow. The greens are warm and cold, depending on how much sunlight they get. The deep blue of the distant ocean contrasts sharply with the breaking wave in the sunlit foreground. Even the crashing surf, as it hits the rocks, forms a pattern of light and shade as the sun hits one part and throws the rest into shadow. The sky, all in a lighter key, melts away into the distance to a warm robin's egg blue, covered in part by scattered clouds, which are again shaped in terms of light and shade. So many differences in color to discern. So many different values to determine. *Collection, Mrs. John L. Coon, Framingham Centre, Massachusetts.*

STORM OVER LANESVILLE, *oil, 40 x 50.* This large oil had its beginning in a detailed pencil drawing of the building structure. Later, a 12 x 16 oil sketch was painted in sunlight. This sketch determined the placing of the barn in relation to the sky, sea, and land areas. The picture looked undistinguished and factual so far. Then I caught an unexpected glimpse of the same subject in a storm. A few hurried notes on the spot resulted in a watercolor back home in the studio, embodying the somber color scheme. The dominant mood of the painting thus achieved, it remained only to create the canvas shown here, using all the available information gathered so far on the way. (It is sad to relate that, in the name of progress, the barn has since been torn down and a housing development now occupies the spot.) *Collection, Converse Memorial Library, Malden, Massachusetts.*

THE SWIRLING FLOOD, *oil, 25 x 30.* Action is the dominant note in this picture: the crashing foam hitting the rocks; the oncoming wave behind, building up for another thunderous blow; and in the foreground, the swirling flood of white foam, still in violent motion, never really settling down before the next explosion smothers it again with tons of moving waters. The student will note that the sky is somewhat subdued; this quiet contrast gives greater emphasis to the action of the sea. Too much action all over the canvas tends to confusion. When this occurs, it indicates that the painter could not decide which interested him most, the sky or the sea. One should complement the other, and their relationship appear inevitable. Warm grays and greens predominate in this painting, and it is, on the whole, painted in a low key. *Collection, Amherst College.*

MOON MAGIC, *oil, 24 x 30.* A glance at the shimmering light of the moon over the sea and shoreline reveals that there is much more color here than in most night paintings. From the moment it first rises above the ocean as a reddish orange disc, the moon changes color. As it ascends upward, it soon becomes almost wholly orange; then, more slowly, the orange turns to a golden yellow, and hours later, to a pale yellow until, finally, the moon shows cold and silver white directly overhead. So each color phase of the moon's climb heavenward presents a different set of conditions for the painter to work with. *Moon Magic* clearly indicates the yellow orange period; in what might be called the supporting cast of colors, we can observe various shades of blue, green, violet, and red—in fact, almost the whole spectrum. (Note that these observations are confined to the eastern seaboard of North America.) *Collection, Dr. Clyde Woodworth, Beverly, Massachusetts.*

CAPE ANN MOONLIGHT, oil, 25 x 30. From a viewpoint close to the water's edge and facing the moon path, the painter observes that the spray thrown into the air becomes a silhouette against the light behind it. A shadow also is cast toward the observer, its contour depending on the height and shape of the spray itself and the relative nearness of the moon to the horizon. The silhouette and the shadow forms are important factors in creating an interesting picture pattern. The student with a sense of design has in these circumstances unlimited opportunity to exercise his imaginative ability. *Courtesy of Frank McQuestern, Marblehead, Mass.*

Index